WHAT
WE ARE
in
Christ

WHAT
WE ARE
in
Christ

E. W. KENYON

WHITAKER
HOUSE

What We Are In Christ

Kenyon's Gospel Publishing Society
P.O. Box 973
Lynnwood, WA 98046-0973
www.kenyons.org

ISBN: 978-1-64123-805-2
Printed in the United States of America
© 2022 by Kenyon's Gospel Publishing Society

Whitaker House
1030 Hunt Valley Circle
New Kensington, PA 15068
www.whitakerhouse.com

Library of Congress Cataloging-in-Publication Data (Pending)

1 2 3 4 5 6 7 8 9 10 11 **ᴜ** 29 28 27 26 25 24 23 22

CONTENTS

INTRODUCTION:
WHAT WE WERE;
WHAT WE ARE IN CHRIST

To most of us, what we were before we found Christ so dominates our minds, so rules us, that we forget what we are now in Him.

We belittle our redemption and we magnify our failures.

Our weakness is ever with us.

We have forgotten that He is ever with us.

We have the "cross" religion rather than the resurrected life of the Son of God.

If we would persistently fix our thoughts upon *what we are in Christ* and what Christ is doing for us at the right hand of the Father, it would lift us out of weakness and failure, into His strength.

Set your mind on things that are above, where Christ is seated at the right hand of God. (See Colossians 3:1–2.)

1

IN CHRIST

"In Christ" is one of the key expressions in the Epistles.

Few have understood all that the Spirit meant when this expression was used by Paul.

You see, there are two expressions used: "In Christ" and "Christ in us."

"In Christ" is our legal standing.

It is what He has done for us in redemption, what He has done for us in the courthouse of heaven.

When we speak of our being "In Christ," that place began historically on the cross.

Jesus was never a substitute until He hung there.

He identified Himself with us when He took a physical body.

We did not become identified with Him until He hung on the cross and God laid our sin upon Him.

So the expression "In Christ" is the legal side of our redemption.

We were "in Him" in the mind of justice when He was nailed to the cross.

We were "in Him" when sin was laid upon Him. It was our sin.

We were "in Him" when He went down into the place of suffering.

We were "in Him" during those awful hours when He was separated from God and under condemnation, when the judgment for our sins fell heavily upon Him.

We were "in Him" when He paid the price and God legally justified Him, made Him righteous, and made Him *"alive in the spirit."*

> *Christ also suffered for sins once, the righteous for the unrighteous, that he might bring us to God; being put to death in the flesh, but made alive in the spirit.*
>
> (1 Peter 3:18 ASV)

We were "in Him" when He conquered the dark host of hell.

We were "in Him" when He put His heel upon the neck of Satan and took from him the keys of death and hades.

We were "in Him" when He rose triumphantly over all the host of the enemy.

We were "in Him" when He ascended from Olivet with His own blood into the holy of holies and there poured that blood on the mercy seat before the throne of God.

We were "in Him" when He sat down on the right hand of the majesty on high.

We were "in Him" until His work was finished.

We were "in Him" until He was seated in the highest place in the universe.

We are "in Him" today, for Paul tells us God *raised us up with him, and made us to sit with him in the heavenly places, in Christ Jesus*" (Ephesians 2:6 asv).

We are "in Him" in this sense. This is the legal side.

This is the courthouse side of the plan of redemption.

When the Father looks upon us, He invariably looks upon us as "in Christ" legally equal with our substitute.

Whatever He attempts to do in us experientially is on legal grounds.

This legal position in Christ guarantees an experiential fellowship with the Lord that will enable us to enter into any spiritual fellowship this side of heaven that will glorify the Father.

Our position is limitless.

All that He is to us legally, He can be experientially.

When I speak about being "in Christ," I mean that we are in all fullness, all might, grace, authority, and dominion that Christ is in Himself.

When you speak about being "in Christ," that is "as Christ."

It is identification in the holiest, highest spiritual sense.

It is a oneness with Him that absolutely beggars any oral description.

These two wonderful words, "in Christ," cover it. You see, the fact that we are "in Christ" means that from heaven's point of view, Satan cannot reach us, nor touch us. His power is absolutely destroyed as far as we are concerned.

When Satan does touch us, it must surprise all heaven to think that such a thing could take place.

Satan must look upon it as a satanic miracle that he can break through the defenses of God and put diseases and sickness upon us and bring us under condemnation.

You see, there are two kinds of miracles: the miracles of God wrought by faith, and the miracles of Satan wrought by hate and unbelief on our part.

The Father is expecting us to occupy our position "in Christ," where there is no condemnation, where we stand complete in Him, where His fullness and completeness become ours, and where the very strength of Christ becomes ours.

I can do all things through Christ who strengthens me.
(Philippians 4:13)

We are in a place where all grace abounds, where we are in the very grasp of omnipotence.

You see, there is no such thing as failure. There is no such thing as being defeated when one really knows that he is "in Christ," for we were "in Him" in all His marvelous victories in redemption.

We are "in Him" now, seated in the highest place in the universe. All it requires is simple faith on our part to bring the power of God to bear upon our needs, whether for spirit, soul, body, finances, or deliverance. Our God is our very ally.

2

CHRIST IN US

"In Christ" is the place for security.

"Christ in us" is the ground for joy and peace that passes understanding.

There are sixteen Scriptures that speak of Christ's ministry and work in us. I can only refer you to a few of them, but they are tremendous in their possibilities for the believer.

> I have been crucified with Christ; it is no longer I who live, but Christ lives in me; and the life which I now live in the flesh I live by faith in the Son of God, who loved me and gave Himself for me.   (Galatians 2:20)

The One with whom Paul was crucified, the One who loved him and gave Himself up for him, now dwells in him.

One can hardly take it in.

Here is unveiled to us the most beautiful, thrilling revelation—that this Christ, who loved us and gave Himself for us, has come into these bodies and made them His home!

There is a challenge as well as a promise in this Scripture:

Do you not know that your body is the temple of the Holy Spirit who is in you, whom you have from God, and you are not your own?   (1 Corinthians 6:19)

These frail bodies of ours that have been sin-touched and disease-marked are His tabernacles. They are His home, His place of abode. He lives in these bodies now.

Who can estimate what that means?

The same power that wrought in the dead body of Jesus is resident in me. (See Ephesians 1:19–20.)

Speaking by the Spirit, Paul said, *"For it is God who works in you both to will and to do for His good pleasure"* (Philippians 2:13).

God at work within me, in my body, in your body.

When we grasp this, disease has lost its power and its place.

Disease cannot do much when you are actually conscious of the indwelling presence.

John says:

*You are of God, little children, and have overcome them,
because He who is in you is greater than he who is in the
world.* (1 John 4:4)

The great, mighty Omnipotent Creator God, who spoke
worlds into being, dwells in these bodies of ours.

You see, when God comes in to take possession of us, He
can think through our minds, love through our affections, and
will through our wills.

He can embed Himself, so to speak, in our spirits, and
through our spirits dominate our spiritual and physical life.

He can dominate over the members of our bodies until
the words of our mouths and the meditation of our hearts will
be acceptable in His sight, until we live and love and have our
being in Him.

Can't you see how mighty it makes us?

Can't you see why Paul said he was independent of
circumstances?

Can't you understand why the Spirit said, *"All things work
together for good to those who love God, to those who are the called
according to His purpose"* (Romans 8:28)? That is us, we who
are in Christ.

We are more than conquerors; we are more than victors;
we are more than overcomers through this marvelous, matchless grace of God, the indwelling God of all grace.

3

WE WERE DEAD IN SIN

Y ou were dead through your trespasses and sins.

> And you He made alive, who were dead in trespasses and sins, in which you once walked according to the course of this world, according to the prince of the power of the air, the spirit who now works in the sons of disobedience, among whom also we all once conducted ourselves in the lusts of our flesh, fulfilling the desires of the flesh and of the mind, and were by nature children of wrath.
>
> (Ephesians 2:1–3)

The word *"dead"* has reference to our spirits.

We had partaken of spiritual death, Satan's nature.

We walked according to the course of this age that is ruled by *"the prince of the power of the air."*

Satan sustains a threefold relationship to man.

Satan is the spiritual father of man.

You are of your father the devil. (John 8:44)

In this the children of God and the children of the devil are manifest: Whoever does not practice righteousness is not of God, nor is he who does not love his brother.
(1 John 3:10)

Satan is not only the spiritual father of this world, but he is the prince that rules the political world.

The ruler of this world is coming, and he has nothing in Me. (John 14:30)

As the ruler of the world, Satan's mind dominates the mind of the world.

In whom the god of this world hath blinded the minds of the unbelieving. (2 Corinthians 4:4 ASV)

He is not only the spiritual father of the political rulers of this world, but he is the god of this world.

Man is worshipping Satan.

It is a master stroke of Satan to get the church to believe in his philosophy rather than in God's Word.

We have many men today who are teaching the philosophy of Satan rather than the Word of God.

At that time you were without Christ, being aliens from the commonwealth of Israel and strangers from the covenants of promise, having no hope and without God in the world. (Ephesians 2:12)

They were not only spiritually dead, subjects of Satan, with Satan's nature dominating them, but they were without a hope, hopeless—and without God, godless, and in the world.

All this shows the utter helplessness of the man outside of Christ to stand in the Father's presence without condemnation.

But God, who is rich in mercy, because of His great love with which He loved us, even when we were dead in trespasses, made us alive together with Christ (by grace you have been saved). (Ephesians 2:4–5)

4

WE ARE ALIVE IN CHRIST

We have seen the great need of a redemption that would deliver us from our union by nature with the enemy, and his dominion over us.

That redemption was planned by God, wrought by Christ, and brought to us by His Spirit through His own Word.

> *But God, who is rich in mercy, because of His great love with which He loved us, even when we were dead in trespasses, made us alive together with Christ.*
>
> (Ephesians 2:4–5)

In the mind of the Father then, when Christ was made alive, we were made alive.

That became operative within us when we accepted Christ as Savior.

You notice that we were not only made alive with Christ, but we were justified with Christ.

Jesus our Lord…was delivered up because of our offenses, and was raised because of our justification.

(Romans 4:24–25)

We were declared righteous when Christ was declared righteous.

When the heart sees this clearly, it is emancipation and deliverance. It is *"together with Christ."* It is utter identification with Him.

Then He says, *"By grace you have been saved"* (Ephesians 2:5).

And raised us up with him, and made us to sit with him in the heavenly places, in Christ Jesus. (Ephesians 2:6 ASV)

The expression, *"Raised us up with him,"* spells out in letters of light our deliverance from Satan's dominion.

If He raised us up with Him, then we are taken out of satanic bondage.

"And made us to sit with him in the heavenly places, in Christ Jesus."

Jesus, a Man, is seated at the right hand of the Father.

His chair represents absolute dominion over the universe.

He is our representative. We are seated in Him.

We are so utterly identified with Him that, in the mind of the Father, He and we are one.

Oh, that our minds might grasp this. *"By grace you have been saved."*

The Greek word that is translated *"saved"* here is *sozo*, which can be translated "healed.

The new birth is the healing of our spirit.

5

BY GRACE ARE YOU SAVED

It would seem that this is the hardest truth for people to learn.

All phases of Christianity where works are prominent are popular. But where we lay aside every human effort and trust the Word, and the Word alone, a storm of protest arises.

Justification or the new birth must be of grace, through faith.

Receiving the Holy Spirit must be purely of grace, by faith.

How much more will your heavenly Father give the Holy Spirit to those who ask Him! (Luke 11:13)

It does not happen by trying to buy it by consecration and surrender, but by simple faith in His Word.

It is not trusting in our physical senses, but it is trusting in His simple Word.

> *And raised us up together, and made us sit together in the heavenly places in Christ Jesus, that in the ages to come He might show the exceeding riches of His grace in His kindness toward us in Christ Jesus. For by grace you have been saved through faith, and that not of yourselves; it is the gift of God, not of works, lest anyone should boast. For we are His workmanship, created in Christ Jesus for good works, which God prepared beforehand that we should walk in them..* (Ephesians 2:6–10)

For by grace we have been saved. Read it again, carefully.

He made us alive together with Him. He raised us up with Him. He made us to sit with Him. All that we did was to accept that as our own—and it was ours. We did nothing to earn it; rather, it was a gift from God.

> *Now to him who works, the wages are not counted as grace but as debt. But to him who does not work but believes on Him who justifies the ungodly, his faith is accounted for righteousness.* (Romans 4:4–5)

If you work and struggle for your salvation, and pay a price for the Holy Spirit, then you receive the Holy Spirit as a payment on a debt for your work.

But you receive the Holy Spirit as a gift of grace. You receive the answer to your prayer as a gift of grace. You receive your healing as a gift.

It is all of grace.

"Not of works, lest anyone should boast."

It is given *"to him who does not work but believes on Him who justifies the ungodly."*

This gift of God is *"not of works, that no man should glory"* (Ephesians 2:9 ASV).

It is not of works, but it is all of grace through faith.

6

WE ARE HIS WORKMANSHIP

This is almost contradictory to modern teaching.

You would think, to hear men and women testify, that they were their own workmanship, that by the things that they have surrendered and given up or consecrated, they have become the sons and daughters of God.

> *For we are His workmanship, created in Christ Jesus for good works, which God prepared beforehand that we should walk in them.* (Ephesians 2:10)

We are God's workmanship, created in Christ.

He took us—the raw material, sinners without hope and without life—and poured into us His own very nature, made us His own very sons and daughters by nature.

We had before been by nature the children of wrath.

Now we are by nature God's own sons and daughters. He not only created us in Christ Jesus, but He prepared good works that we should walk in them.

In other words, He made provision whereby every one of us may walk in love, walk by faith.

He made provision whereby the life of Jesus should be reproduced in us, in our daily contact with people.

We are no longer to walk as the heathens walk, in the futility or vanity of their minds, with their hearts blinded or hardened. (See Ephesians 4:17–23.)

But we have not so learned Christ. We have put away, as concerning our former manner of life, the old man.

> *Knowing this, that our old man was crucified with Him, that the body of sin might be done away with, that we should no longer be slaves of sin.* (Romans 6:6)

"The old man which grows corrupt" (Ephesians 4:22) was nailed to the cross in Christ and was buried with Him, was put away.

When Christ arose from the dead, He was free from this old man.

As soon as we take Jesus Christ as our Savior, and come to know what grace really means, we are free too.

You are to walk in the strength and grace of the risen Christ, not by willpower, but by faith in the Word.

"For it is God who works in you" (Philippians 2:13).

7

HE IS OUR PEACE

*Therefore, having been justified by faith, we have peace
with God through our Lord Jesus Christ.*
—Romans 5:1

Here we have peace with God instead of confusion from sin.

This comes when we accept Christ as Savior and Lord, and receive eternal life.

*And the peace of God, which surpasses all understanding,
will guard your hearts and minds through Christ Jesus.*
(Philippians 4:7)

Here is the peace of God.

God's peace, God's holy quietness, comes into the heart of the newborn in Christ.

It is a peace we cannot understand. Jesus is that peace.

"For He Himself is our peace" (Ephesians 2:14).

This is perhaps the greatest blessing that can come to the human heart.

Peace means *utter quietness* and *rest*. It is the rest of faith.

We are no longer afraid of the judgment. We are no longer afraid of death or what man can do to us.

We are not afraid of Satan. We know that he is conquered. We know that we rule over him. We know that he, and his works, are beneath our feet in Christ.

This is the peace that Jesus spoke of in the Gospel of John: *"Peace I leave with you, My peace I give to you"* (John 14:27).

The disciples could not help but recognize how differently Jesus accepted the cross and its suffering than the thieves did who were crucified with Him.

They could not help but notice how utterly quiet, peaceful, and restful He was in the judgment hall of Pilate.

So when He says, "My peace I leave with you," at once, our heart reaches out for it.

We are surrounded by Pilate's judgment halls everywhere. The scourge of tongues and the bitterness of the world mind confronts us everywhere.

We need this peace.

These things I have spoken to you, that in Me you may have peace. In the world you will have tribulation; but be of good cheer, I have overcome the world.   (John 16:33)

THE ONE NEW MAN

If this was purely the dream of the man called Paul, then he could write novels or dramas such as no Dickens or Shakespeare ever approximated.

But it was not the dream of Paul; it was the dream of the Father God.

> *So as to create in Himself one new man from the two, thus making peace, and that He might reconcile them both to God in one body through the cross, thereby putting to death the enmity.* (Ephesians 2:15–16)

There was enmity between the Jew under the law and the gentile without the law.

Now that enmity is slain, when the Jew and the gentile are born again, both of them come into the body of Christ, where they are *one new man*.

This new creation teaching is the master stroke of God.

Therefore, if anyone is in Christ, he is a new creation; old things have passed away; behold, all things have become new. Now all things are of God, who has reconciled us to Himself through Jesus Christ, and has given us the ministry of reconciliation.   (2 Corinthians 5:17–18)

If God had simply forgiven man for what he had done, and did nothing more, man would continue to commit sin.

But God does not forgive the sinner. He makes him a new creation. He remits and wipes out all that the sinner has ever done. He stops a man being a sinner and makes him a saint by the new creation.

He imparts to him His own nature. Old things pass away. All things become new in Christ.

And put on the new man, that after God hath been created in righteousness and holiness of truth.

(Ephesians 4:24 asv)

This new creation is made out of righteousness, so he is righteousness.

He is made out of holiness, so he is holy.

He is made out of truth, so he is real.

The Father actually unveils His very genius in this new birth.

We are the workmanship of God in Christ Jesus.

WHAT WE ARE IN CHRIST

*Being justified freely by His grace through the
redemption that is in Christ Jesus.*
—Romans 3:24

Our redemption is *in Christ*. No one can rob us of it.

It was God's own work. He is satisfied with it.

In Him we have redemption through His blood, the forgiveness of sins, according to the riches of His grace.

(Ephesians 1:7)

It is according to *"the riches of His grace."*

Not a beggarly redemption, barely redeemed, but a vast, God-sized redemption.

He has delivered us from the power of darkness and conveyed us into the kingdom of the Son of His love, in whom we have redemption through His blood, the forgiveness of sins.   (Colossians 1:13–14)

It translated us out of Satan's realm into His own love kingdom.

In this translation, He made us sons.

For you were bought at a price.   (1 Corinthians 6:20)

Knowing that you were not redeemed with corruptible things, like silver or gold, from your aimless conduct received by tradition from your fathers, but with the precious blood of Christ, as of a lamb without blemish and without spot.   (1 Peter 1:18–19)

Redeemed with the blood of Christ. Redeemed from Satan.

Redeemed from the claims of justice. The price was paid to justice.

You were bought at a price; do not become slaves of men.
                                    (1 Corinthians 7:23)

Stand fast therefore in the liberty by which Christ has made us free, and do not be entangled again with a yoke of bondage.   (Galatians 5:1)

Stand fast in your liberty.

God set you free. You are free.

Satan has no claim on you. Justice has no claim on you. Neither Satan nor justice can hold you.

You are a new creation, a child of God.

You have been redeemed from the hand of your enemy.

You are to take this fact seriously. You are to order your life accordingly.

For sin shall not have dominion over you.

(Romans 6:14)

Satan was defeated by the Master. That defeat stripped him of his ability to take you captive again, without your cooperation.

You see, there are two sides to redemption.

One is Jesus paying the price of your redemption, satisfying the claims of justice.

And the other side is Jesus defeating your enemy and breaking his dominion.

Having disarmed principalities and powers, He made a public spectacle of them, triumphing over them in it.

(Colossians 2:15)

Here we have a picture of Jesus putting off from Himself the hosts of hell, breaking their dominion, and rising from the dead.

Inasmuch then as the children have partaken of flesh and blood, He Himself likewise shared in the same, that through death He might destroy him who had the power of death, that is, the devil.   (Hebrews 2:14)

10

WE ARE NEW CREATIONS

We are "in Christ" people. We are redeemed. We are free in Christ.

Neither justice, nor Satan, has any claim on us!

The sin nature that God covered in the Jew is gone. We are a new creation.

> *Therefore, if anyone is in Christ, he is a new creation; old things have passed away; behold, all things have become new.* (2 Corinthians 5:17)

If we are in Christ, we are new creations. The Holy Spirit has given birth to us. We are the "born of God."

We are born "from above." (See John 3:3–8.) We are of God.

> *You are of God, little children.* (1 John 4:4)

For we are His workmanship, created in Christ Jesus for good works.   (Ephesians 2:10)

We are His workmanship, a creation in Christ. We are God's own creation.

The sin that the blood of animals covered is put away.

Knowing this, that our old man was crucified with Him, that the body of sin might be done away with, that we should no longer be slaves of sin.   (Romans 6:6)

The old man, the body of sin, is done away in the new creation. The sin nature is gone. The new nature is in its place.

So many of us have tried to get rid of this *old nature.*

We did not know that it was done away in the new creation.

This new creation is the life and nature of God imparted to our spirits.

The thing called the *old man*—theologically the *Adam nature*—was spiritual death that had possession of our spirits.

When we were made alive, made new creations, that nature was done away.

Because we are tempted and in our babyhood state, before our minds are renewed, we do unseemly things, some of us have been led to believe that we still have sin in us.

There is only one place for sin to reside and that is in our spirits. But our spirits have been recreated. The sin nature has been taken out of us.

We know that we have passed from death to life, because we love the brethren.   (1 John 3:14)

Satan's nature is gone. God's nature has come in.

And that ye be renewed in the spirit of your mind, and put on the new man, that after God hath been created in righteousness and holiness of truth.

(Ephesians 4:23–24)

A new man is *"created in righteousness and holiness of truth."*

This new creation is of God. It is God's own nature.

So, we know we are His own.

WE ARE THE RIGHTEOUSNESS OF GOD

We are redeemed. Satan and justice have no claims against us.

God Himself in Christ satisfied the claims of justice and in Christ conquered Satan, delivering us from his authority.

We are in Christ.

Being in Christ, we are new creations.

Being new creations, we have but one Lord—Jesus.

Satan has no authority over us. We are no longer afraid of Satan or what he can do. We are not afraid of ourselves as this self is a new creation.

We are not afraid of God, as we have been reconciled to Him in the death of His Son.

Now all things are of God, who has reconciled us to Himself through Jesus Christ, and has given us the ministry of reconciliation.　　　(2 Corinthians 5:18)

Being reconciled, we have fellowship with the Father and with His Son, Jesus Christ.

Reconciliation is another word for fellowship.

Being justified freely by His grace through the redemption that is in Christ Jesus, whom God set forth as a propitiation by His blood, through faith, to demonstrate His righteousness, because in His forbearance God had passed over the sins that were previously committed, to demonstrate at the present time His righteousness, that He might be just and the justifier of the one who has faith in Jesus.　　　(Romans 3:24–26)

The word *justified* means "made righteous."

Then we have been declared righteous by His grace.

Another translation reads:

For the shewing forth of His righteousness in the present time, for His being righteous, and declaring him righteous who [is] of the faith of Jesus.　　　(Romans 3:26 YLT)

Jesus put sin away by the sacrifice of Himself.

But now, once at the end of the ages, He has appeared to put away sin by the sacrifice of Himself. (Hebrews 9:26)

You note the word *"Himself"* that comes out again and again, showing that our righteousness is a God-wrought thing.

> *He made Him who knew no sin to be sin for us, that we might become the righteousness of God in Him.*
> (2 Corinthians 5:21)

God made Him to be sin *"that we might become the righteousness of God in Him."*

By the new birth, this is brought to pass.

> *But of Him you are in Christ Jesus, who became for us wisdom from God—and righteousness and sanctification and redemption.*   (1 Corinthians 1:30)

God makes Jesus our righteousness.

> *But my righteous one will live by faith.*
> (Hebrews 10:38 NIV)

We are His righteous ones.

It is imperative that we take our place and act our part.

God has made us righteous.

We must act as though we were righteous. God cannot bless unless we take our place.

You notice God has become the righteousness of the man who has faith in Jesus.

He not only declares us righteous, but now, by His great grace, He becomes our righteousness.

12

WE ARE SONS OF GOD

We are redeemed. We are new creations. We are the righteousness of God.

All of this is wrought of God.

He calls us, "My righteous ones who walk by faith."

Now we are to take our place as sons. What grace!

Once, we were sons of Satan.

Now, we are sons of God, by a new birth based upon legal grounds.

> *For as many as are led by the Spirit of God, these are sons of God.* (Romans 8:14)

This is the climax of God's revelation to Paul—becoming sons of God.

God bears witness that the thing is done. You are born into His family.

For as many as received Him, to them, He gives the right to become children of God.

> *But as many as received Him, to them He gave the right to become children of God, to those who believe in His name: who were born, not of blood, nor of the will of the flesh, nor of the will of man, but of God.* (John 1:12–13)

On the ground of what God did in Christ, everyone has a right to sonship privileges.

> *And I will receive you. I will be a Father to you, and you shall be My sons and daughters, says the* LORD *Almighty.* (2 Corinthians 6:17–18)

God will take His place. You take yours.

> *Beloved, now we are children of God.* (1 John 3:2)

We are sons now, with a son's rights, a son's authority.

> *For you are all sons of God through faith in Christ Jesus.* (Galatians 3:26)

Now take your place as a child. Enjoy your rights.

You are welcome in His presence. He loves you. He longs for your fellowship.

If you are sons, God is now your Father. You are in His family.

This is the objective toward which all the purposes of God have been working ever since the fall of man.

If you have never taken your place as a son, if you have never enjoyed the sweet fellowship that belongs to you as a child of God, you have been missing the richest feature in Christianity.

> *God is faithful, by whom you were called into the fellow-ship of His Son, Jesus Christ our Lord.*
>
> (1 Corinthians 1:9)

This fellowship is with the Father.

This only comes in its fullness and richness when the mind is renewed through the Word by the Spirit.

He will be a far-away God to you until you learn to call Him Father and take your place as a child.

13

WE ARE CARED FOR IN CHRIST

We have come into all these vast riches of grace through believing on Jesus and confessing His lordship over us.

> *The LORD is my shepherd; I shall not want. He makes me to lie down in green pastures; He leads me beside the still waters. He restores my soul; He leads me in the paths of righteousness for His name's sake.* (Psalm 23:1–3)

Jesus is your Lord; you shall not want.

He is your caretaker, your own love Lord.

> *And my God shall supply all your need according to His riches in glory by Christ Jesus.* (Philippians 4:19)

My God shall supply all of your needs. This means every need—body, soul, and spirit.

Blessed be the God and Father of our Lord Jesus Christ, who has blessed us with every spiritual blessing in the heavenly places in Christ. (Ephesians 1:3)

He has blessed you with every spiritual blessing in Christ.

All is yours. All has been given you.

Just thank Him for what you need.

Cast all your anxiety on him because he cares for you.
(1 Peter 5:7 NIV)

If anyone loves Me, he will keep My word; and My Father will love him, and We will come to him and make Our home with him. (John 14:23)

Jesus and the Father will come and live with you, make your home theirs.

Therefore do not worry, saying, "What shall we eat?" or "What shall we drink?" or "What shall we wear?" For after all these things the Gentiles seek. For your heavenly Father knows that you need all these things. But seek first the kingdom of God and His righteousness, and all these things shall be added to you. (Matthew 6:31–33)

Your Heavenly Father knows all of your needs and He will give them to you. Therefore, do not be anxious.

If you can learn to put Him first, to trust His Word absolutely, there will come into your heart a new sense of protection and care.

> *Trust in the LORD with all your heart, and lean not on your own understanding; in all your ways acknowledge Him, and He shall direct your paths.* (Proverbs 3:5–6)

The way to have His care and protection is on this road of trust.

No other way makes an appeal to Him.

Your reasoning and arguments only lead to confusion.

Rest quietly in His love. Trust Him utterly in everything, and you will know what it means when He says, *"You will keep him in perfect peace, whose mind is stayed on You, because he trusts in You"* (Isaiah 26:3).

> *Until now you have asked nothing in My name. Ask, and you will receive, that your joy may be full.* (John 16:24)

Here you have the privilege of joining forces with Him, and carrying out His will on the earth.

You can really be a child of God in your daily life.

WHAT CHRIST IS TO ME NOW

You have seen what He has done for you in Christ.

You have seen what He has made you to be in Christ—"redeemed," a "new creation," "the righteousness of God," and "the sons of God." You are cared for by God.

Now we go on to see what God has made Christ to be to us.

"A Savior, who is Christ the Lord" (Luke 2:11). He is the only Savior. God alone can save.

Jesus said to him, "I am the way, the truth, and the life. No one comes to the Father except through Me."

(John 14:6)

And for this reason He is the Mediator of the new covenant. (Hebrews 9:15)

He is the only Mediator, God's appointed One.

Therefore He is also able to save to the uttermost those who come to God through Him, since He always lives to make intercession for them. (Hebrews 7:25)

He is our Intercessor at God's right hand.

But of Him you are in Christ Jesus, who became for us wisdom from God—and righteousness and sanctification and redemption. (1 Corinthians 1:30)

God made Him to be our righteousness, so we can go into the Father's presence without fear.

Our sanctification, redemption, and wisdom—all of this, God made Him to be for us.

The LORD is my light and my salvation; whom shall I fear? The LORD is the strength of my life; of whom shall I be afraid? (Psalm 27:1)

He is our light and salvation. He is the strength of our life.

Jesus said to them, "I am the bread of life. He who comes to Me shall never hunger, and he who believes in Me shall never thirst." (John 6:35)

He is our bread and water of life. He is all we need.

Who Himself bore our sins in His own body on the tree, that we, having died to sins, might live for righteousness—by whose stripes you were healed.

(1 Peter 2:24)

He is our healer and our healing.

Now trust Him for all things. He is everything to you now.

He's a Savior; He has saved you out of your sins. He has saved you from the dominion and power of Satan.

He is your way to walk, to live, to absolutely trust.

He is your reality. And the Spirit Himself will lead you into the reality of Jesus, where prayer will become a living thing, where fellowship will be rich and beautiful.

His life will swallow up your weaknesses. He will be the strength of your life.

Not only this, but He is your great Intercessor. He ever lives at the Father's right hand to make intercession for you.

Your prayers may fail, but His cannot.

Not only is He all this, but He is your great Advocate, who ever sits before the Father on your behalf.

He makes Christianity a living reality.

15

LIVING IN HIM

It was a surprise to the writer to find that the expressions "*in Christ*," "*in whom*," and "*in Him*" occur more than 130 times in the New Testament.

This is the heart of the life in Him.

Here is the secret of faith that conquers, faith that moves mountains.

Here is the secret of the Spirit's guiding us into all reality. The heart craves intimacy with the Lord Jesus and with the Father.

> *In Him we have redemption through His blood, the forgiveness of sins, according to the riches of His grace.*
>
> (Ephesians 1:7)

It is not a beggarly redemption.

It is a God-like redemption by the God who could say, *"Let there be lights in the firmament of the heavens"* (Genesis 1:14), causing the whole starry heavens to leap into being in a single instant.

That is omnipotence. That is beyond human reason. That is where philosophy has never left a footprint. That is like our miraculous redemption. It is *"according to the riches of His grace."*

Not only that, but it is through His blood.

His grace *"He made to abound toward us in all wisdom and prudence"* (Ephesians 1:8).

It is lavish. It is abundant, but it is mixed with wisdom.

Our redemption is a perfect thing. When you know it and enter into it, your heart grows accustomed to it, and there will be ability in your life that you have never known.

> *He has delivered us from the power of darkness and conveyed us into the kingdom of the Son of His love, in whom we have redemption through His blood, the forgiveness of sins.*　　　　　　　　　　　(Colossians 1:13–14)

You are delivered out of the authority of Satan. You are free.

It is in Him that we have our redemption.

You have been delivered out of Satan's dominion.

You have been transferred into the kingdom of His love.

You are free from the dominion of Satan.

The hour will come when you will awaken to the fact that he cannot put disease upon you, that he cannot give you pain and anguish in your body.

The hour will come when you will know that want and poverty are things of the past, as far as you are concerned.

You will shout amid the turbulence and fear of other men, "The Lord is now my shepherd. I shall not want. He makes me to lie down in plenty, in fullness. I am satisfied with Him." (See Psalm 23:1.)

This redemption is real. Satan is defeated. Disease is outlawed. Want is banished.

We are free.

Therefore if the Son makes you free, you shall be free indeed. (John 8:36)

The word *"indeed"* there really means "in reality."

I have come that they may have life, and that they may have it more abundantly. (John 10:10)

What is life? Life is the nature of God.

You may have the Father's nature abundantly. You are in Christ.

You are in the very realm of life.

That life has in it the life that transcends reasoning. It is eternal life.

In John 14:6, Jesus said, *"I am the way, the truth, and the life."* The truth is the reality of God.

He was unveiling to the heart what He can be to us. He can be life to us.

He can be reality to us.

He can fulfill every desire with satisfaction. That is the kind of risen Lord that we have.

> *Stand fast therefore in the liberty by which Christ has made us free, and do not be entangled again with a yoke of bondage.*   (Galatians 5:1)

The gravest danger of the believer is that after he has been made free, he will lapse back into bondage.

When he leaves the realm of the spirit and of faith, he walks in the realm of sight and the senses.

As sense reason gains the supremacy, he loses his joy in the Lord.

We are new creations in Christ Jesus. This is a thrilling truth.

We are just finding out what this can mean to us.

> *Therefore, if anyone is in Christ, he is a new creation; old things have passed away.*   (2 Corinthians 5:17)

Whether you know it or not, this new creation fact means to you all that it means to Jesus and the Father.

Paul's Revelation is filled with new creation truth. It is God's dream for you to enjoy the fullness of this new creation's privileges.

"Old things have passed away." Those old things of bondage, fear, doubt, want, sickness, weakness, and failure are gone.

You say, "That is not possible. These things do not belong to the new creation."

The new creation is just like the Master. He is the Head. You are the body. He is the Vine. You are the branch. As He is, so are you.

Jesus said, *"I am the true vine, and My Father is the vine-dresser…I am the vine, you are the branches"* (John 15:1, 7).

> *Beloved, let us love one another, for love is of God; and everyone who loves is born of God and knows God.*
>
> (1 John 4:7)

Just as long as you deal in doubts and fears, as you sit in judgment on yourself, you will never arrive. You will never enjoy these things.

But if you will act on the Word, take it for granted, and act on it as you would act on a letter from some friend, you will arrive.

Now act upon the Word of God, which cannot be broken.

When God says, *"All things have become new"* (2 Corinthians 5:17), start thinking of yourself as living in this new realm.

16

WE ARE RECONCILED

You have been reconciled to God through Jesus Christ. You have perfect fellowship now.

Oh, the wealth that belongs to you in this new relationship! Dare to act your part!

For we are His workmanship, created in Christ Jesus for good works, which God prepared beforehand that we should walk in them.   (Ephesians 2:10)

If you are His workmanship, you are satisfactory to Him.

He is pleased with you.

We have preached condemnation and sin so long that we do not know how to preach righteousness and tell people what they are in Christ.

When someone does tell them, they feel it is false teaching. They feel that anything is false teaching that does not honor sin and lift it into the place of Christ.

You are God's new man.

Ephesians 2:15 declares He made one new man: "*Having abolished in His flesh the enmity, that is, the law of commandments contained in ordinances, so as to create in Himself one new man from the two, thus making peace.*"

> *And put on the new man, that after God hath been created in righteousness and holiness of truth.*
>
> (Ephesians 4:24 ASV)

The new creation knows but one Lord. Jesus is the Lord of the new creation.

Paul gives us a graphic statement of fact:

> *As you therefore have received Christ Jesus the Lord, so walk in Him, rooted and built up in Him and established in the faith, as you have been taught, abounding in it with thanksgiving.* (Colossians 2:6–7)

What a glorious truth!

No longer are you a weakling. His strength is your strength.

We are so strong that we are to abound in thanksgiving. When we stop abounding in thanksgiving, we deteriorate spiritually.

The LORD is my light and my salvation; whom shall I fear? The LORD is the strength of my life; of whom shall I be afraid? (Psalm 27:1)

The LORD is my shepherd; I shall not want.

(Psalm 23:1)

You swing free from the old prison house of bondage, fear, want, hunger, and cold.

You are out in the freedom of God.

Hebrews 7:25 is Jesus's present attitude toward you: *"Therefore He is also able to save to the uttermost those who come to God through Him, since He always lives to make intercession for them."*

He ever lives to make intercession for you. He is seated at the Father's right hand.

Say it over again, "He ever lives for me."

Just as that wife lives for that man whom she loves, so in a greater measure the Lord Jesus lives for you.

He has only one business and that is living for you.

17

THE GIFT OF RIGHTEOUSNESS

We are His righteousness.

Of all the wealth that is known to the human heart, there is nothing that equals this, that Jesus declares through the apostle Paul that we are His righteousness.

I cannot grasp it.

We are *His righteousness*. How precious we must be to Him! He once became our righteousness. He once declared us righteous by His resurrection from the dead. Now He goes beyond the declaration and makes that declaration a reality.

> *He made Him who knew no sin to be sin for us, that we might become the righteousness of God in Him.*
>   (2 Corinthians 5:21)

But of Him you are in Christ Jesus, who became for us wisdom from God—and righteousness and sanctification and redemption. (1 Corinthians 1:30)

The life which I now live in the flesh I live by faith in the Son of God, who loved me and gave Himself for me.
(Galatians 2:20)

He loved me. He gave Himself up for me. What love is revealed here!

He not only redeemed me and sanctified me, but now before heaven, He says, "I am that man's redemption. I am that man's sanctification."

Then I can hear His voice rise to notes of utter triumph when He shouts, "I am his righteousness and his wisdom."

This is all His work. It is not of man's works lest he should say, "I had a share in that."

Your repenting, crying, and weeping had nothing to do with your righteousness or your redemption.

You stand complete in Him, in all the fullness of His great, matchless life.

Here is the climax of the revelation of our redemption: *"Who shall lay anything to the charge of God's elect?"* (Romans 8:33 ASV).

You are God's elect. Jesus and the Father have elected you. Now He says, "Who shall lay anything to the charge of My own son, My daughter?"

There is only one person of any standing before the Supreme Court who could lay anything to your charge. That is Jesus—and He will not do it.

> *Who is he who condemns? It is Christ who died, and furthermore is also risen, who is even at the right hand of God, who also makes intercession for us.* (Romans 8:34)

Can't you see the wealth of your position?

Can't you see the riches of the glory of your inheritance in Christ?

You are in Him. All that He planned in Jesus is a heart reality now.

There is no condemnation. There is no judgment for you. There is no fear of death. Because death is simply swinging the portals open for you to march in triumph into the presence of your Father.

His Word grips the heart. "*There is no fear in love; but perfect love casts out fear*" (1 John 4:18). In Christ, we have received eternal life, the nature of our Father.

That nature is love. That love is perfect. Our human love is imperfect, but God's love is *agape*, the thing that makes life beautiful. You may not perfectly understand or perfectly enter into it, but it is His perfect love, and it is all yours now.

For as the body is one and has many members, but all the members of that one body, being many, are one body, so also is Christ.   (1 Corinthians 12:12)

We are so one with Him that we are called "the Christ." The church is called "the Christ." He is the Vine. You are the branch. *"I am the vine, you are the branches. He who abides in Me, and I in him, bears much fruit"* (John 15:5). As the branch is to the vine, so are you to the heart of Jesus. You are utterly one with Him.

All this time, you have been thinking about your sin, about your weakness, and your failings. Hear Him whisper to your heart now: *"There is therefore now no condemnation to those who are in Christ Jesus"* (Romans 8:1).

If you are born again, you are in Christ. You are a conqueror. You are free from condemnation. You are the righteousness of God in Him. You are the fullness of God in Him. You are complete in Him. The wealth of His glory, the wealth of His riches, has never been fully expressed.

You are righteous. There is no sin consciousness for you. There is no inferiority complex for you.

You are now in Christ, the very righteousness of God.

You can use the name of Jesus without fear.

You can do as Peter did for the lame man at the temple gate, telling him, *"Silver and gold I do not have, but what I do have I give you: In the name of Jesus Christ of Nazareth, rise up and walk"* (Acts 3:6). You can walk free.

Whatever you ask the Father in My name He will give you.   (John 16:23)

If you abide in Me, and My words abide in you, you will ask what you desire, and it shall be done for you.
                                                              (John 15:7)

These promises are yours now.

You are in Him. He is in you. His Word abides in you.

You are His righteousness. You are His life. You are all and all in Him.

You can do His works now.

He who believes in Me, the works that I do he will do also; and greater works than these he will do, because I go to My Father. And whatever you ask in My name, that I will do, that the Father may be glorified in the Son.
                                                              (John 14:12–13)

You take your place, play the part. Use the name to heal the sick.

His death was not in vain. His suffering was not in vain.

You stand complete in His completeness.

You are filled with His fullness. His grace is yours.

18

WHAT WE CONFESS

Seeing then that we have a great High Priest who has passed through the heavens, Jesus the Son of God, let us hold fast our confession.
—Hebrews 4:14

This Scripture can become a reality in you. The word here is not "profession" but "confession." Christianity is called the *great confession*.

Your confession is that you are in Christ.

All we have said to you in these lessons is a reality to you.

You hold fast to it.

The adversary will try to make you deny your confession. He will try to make you confess another thing rather than this.

He will try to make you confess weakness and failure and want.

But you hold fast to your confession that "my God does supply every need of mine." (See Philippians 4:19.) You stand by that confession.

I can do all things through Christ who strengthens me.
(Philippians 4:13)

You make the declaration that He is the strength of your life.

Who Himself bore our sins in His own body on the tree,
that we, having died to sins, might live for righteousness—
by whose stripes you were healed.   (1 Peter 2:24)

You died unto sins with Christ on that cross; you arose to walk in righteousness, and by His stripes, you are healed.

When Jesus arose from the dead, healing belonged to you.

You hold fast to your confession in the face of every assault of the enemy.

You rebuke it in the name of Jesus.

You walk in the way of righteousness. That is the way of victory.

That is the way where you cast out demons and disease in the name of Jesus.

Every disease that has afflicted a Christian could have been healed if there had been anyone who had dared to walk in righteousness toward that believer and who would have dared walk in the fullness of his privileges in Christ.

The devil could have been driven out and healing could have been his.

> *For we have not a chief priest unable to sympathise with our infirmities, but [one] tempted in all things in like manner—apart from sin; we may come near, then, with freedom, to the throne of the grace.*
>
> (Hebrews 4:15–16 YLT)

You are invited to come now to the throne room and sit with the Master and with the Father.

You are to come in with the Master and with the Father.

You are to come boldly. Don't come creeping in. Don't come in confessing your sins, bewailing your weakness and failures.

Put on the new garment. Dress fittingly to appear before the throne.

You are the sons and daughters of God Almighty, without condemnation.

You will "obtain mercy and find grace to help in time of need" (Hebrews 4:16).

If we realized what we were in Christ, and knew that we had the ability to be what God says we are, our lives would be transformed in a week.

We do not know what redemption and the new creation have made us.

We do not know what we are to the Father's heart and what He is to us.

Most of us are theological Christians instead of Bible Christians.

We have theological experiences and are ever attempting to square the Word with those experiences.

We have been taught that there is no truth beyond our creed.

We lock our people in a creed, making them prisoners of the theories of men born a hundred years ago.

The creed Christian is not a Bible Christian. Each creed must have the Bible translated to fit it.

We have discovered a Christ who is greater than the creeds, a redemption that is greater than the creeds, and a new birth that bursts the bonds of creedal Christianity and sets the prisoners free.

We are discovering a type of Christianity that is better than the creeds, better than anything to which the creeds have given birth.

The creeds, beautiful though they are, are largely born of sense knowledge.

19

WE ARE REDEEMED

Through the redemption that is in Christ Jesus, whom
God set forth as a propitiation by His blood, through
faith, to demonstrate His righteousness.
—Romans 3:24–25

Our redemption, our Redeemer, is Christ. No one can rob you of your redemption.

If you take Christ as your Savior, He becomes your redemption. You become independent of man.

Your redemption was God's own work, and He Himself is satisfied with what He did in Christ.

For we are His workmanship, created in Christ Jesus
for good works, which God prepared beforehand that we
should walk in them. (Ephesians 2:10)

> *In Him we have redemption through His blood, the forgiveness of sins, according to the riches of His grace.*
>
> (Ephesians 1:7)

If you have your redemption, you are redeemed.

Your redemption was through the blood of Jesus Christ. You have the remission of your trespasses.

Notice first: you have your redemption in Christ. It is through the blood of the Son of God.

You have the remission of all that you ever did before you became a Christian.

This redemption is according to the riches of His grace.

It is a perfect, a complete redemption.

It is not a beggarly redemption, but a vast God-sized redemption that glorified God and glorified Christ and honors every man who embraces it.

God *"has delivered us from the power of darkness"* (Colossians 1:13).

That is Satan's power, his authority. If we are delivered out of his authority, he can no longer reign over us.

Yet the great body of the church is living under the dominion of the adversary as though it had never been born again.

What is the matter?

The creed to which we have subscribed has no actual redemption in it.

It has robbed the church of its own redemption by setting stakes of limitation.

The Father...delivered us out of the power of darkness, and translated us into the kingdom of the Son of his love; in whom we have our redemption, the forgiveness of our sins. (Colossians 1:12–14 ASV)

Put it in the first person. *You* are the one who has been delivered. *You* are the one who has been translated into God's kingdom and God's family.

In Christ, you have your redemption, the remission of everything that you ever did.

The new birth settles the problem of your sin nature. It gives you the nature of God and takes the nature of the adversary out of you.

All you ever did is wiped out.

All you ever were has been destroyed.

You are now an actual child of God, just as Jesus was in His earth walk.

You have the same standing that Jesus had because Jesus *is* your standing.

He has become your righteousness. God Himself becomes your standing.

He Himself is righteous and He is the righteousness of those who have faith in Jesus. (See Romans 3:26.)

You have faith in Jesus as your substitute.

So God has become your righteousness.

When you believe this, you will come out of bondage, weakness, and failure into the fullness of this new life in Christ.

You are the sons of God.

You are heirs of God and joint heirs with Jesus Christ. You are redeemed.

"For you were bought at a price" (1 Corinthians 6:20). That price was the blood of Christ.

There is no joint ownership between Christ and the devil. You either belong to the devil or you belong to Christ. Christ purchased you with His own blood.

> *For you know that it was not with perishable things such as silver or gold that you were redeemed from the empty way of life handed down to you from your ancestors, but with the precious blood of Christ, a lamb without blemish or defect.* (1 Peter 1:18–19 NIV)

It is the blood of the Lamb without spot.

You stand before the Father now as a redeemed one, without condemnation.

The blood of Jesus Christ, God's Son, redeemed you. Every claim of justice has been paid. Jesus met the demands of justice and satisfied them. You are free.

20

WE ARE FREE

You were bought at a price; do not become slaves of men.
—1 Corinthians 7:23

This means do not become the bondservant or slave of the theories of men, the creeds of men.

Man here means the man who walks in the senses.

You crown Jesus as the Lord of your life.

There is no other bondage but the bondage of love.

Therefore if the Son makes you free, you shall be free indeed. (John 8:36)

You are free from Satan's dominion. You are a new creation, a child of God.

You have been redeemed from the hand of your enemy.

You are to take this fact seriously. You are to order your life accordingly.

"Sin shall not have dominion over you" (Romans 6:14). Satan was defeated by your Master. That defeat stripped him of his ability to take you captive without your cooperation.

The two phases of Christ's ministry in redemption are: Jesus paying the price of your redemption; and defeating your enemy and setting you free.

> *Having disarmed principalities and powers, He made a public spectacle of them, triumphing over them in it.*
>
> (Colossians 2:15)

Jesus triumphed over the adversary. His triumph was your triumph. He defeated the enemy for you.

That battle was your battle.

He was not fighting for Himself.

> *Inasmuch then as the children have partaken of flesh and blood, He Himself likewise shared in the same, that through death He might destroy him who had the power of death, that is, the devil.*   (Hebrews 2:14)

He set you free. You are free. You are redeemed by God Himself.

A NEW CREATION

Next I want you to notice that you are a new creation. This truth has never been given its place.

All we have been taught was that God forgave us our sins and that by a second work of grace, sin was eradicated from us.

But if we did wrong ignorantly or intelligently, we had to be justified again.

That justification permitted us to be justified with the devil's nature in us.

Another view is that God was unable to take out Satan's nature when He gave us His nature.

So that when we were born again, we had God's nature *and* the devil's nature in us. We warred against the devil's nature in us.

They said we would be free when we died. Satan is the author of death. That would make Satan your savior. Far be the thought!

All of these teachings belong to sense knowledge's interpretation of the Word.

Spiritual things are spiritually understood.

Now we have received, not the spirit of the world, but the Spirit who is from God, that we might know the things that have been freely given to us by God.

(1 Corinthians 2:12)

The first thing that is given to you after redemption is a new creation.

This Scripture must ever stand as the key to this wonderful truth:

> *Therefore, if anyone is in Christ, he is a new creation; old things have passed away; behold, all things have become new. Now all things are of God, who has reconciled us to Himself through Jesus Christ, and has given us the ministry of reconciliation, that is, that God was in Christ reconciling the world to Himself, not imputing their trespasses to them, and has committed to us the word of reconciliation.* (2 Corinthians 5:17–19)

You are a new creation.

The devil's nature has been taken out of you.

God's nature has taken its place. You are reconciled to the Father. You are brought into fellowship with the Father. Everything you were stopped being.

All you were in Satan stopped being.

The old things of weakness and failure are passed. This new creation has no memory of a past creation. You are newly born.

You are a new species.

You are a new creation created in Christ Jesus.

The Jew was blood covered because his nature was antagonistic toward God.

We are not blood covered. We are made new creations. We are cleansed by the blood. We need not be covered.

We can stand uncovered—free from sin consciousness in His presence just as Jesus did in His earth walk.

The Holy Spirit has given birth to us. We are born of God.

Of His own will He brought us forth by the word of truth, that we might be a kind of firstfruits of His creatures.

(James 1:18)

You are of God, little children.   (1 John 4:4)

For we are His workmanship, created in Christ Jesus.

(Ephesians 2:10)

All of this drives us to the conclusion that this new creation is something that God Himself has wrought out and that we are now just what He says we are: the very sons of God.

The man of sin is done away with in the new creation.

Knowing this, that our old man was crucified with Him, that the body of sin might be done away with, that we should no longer be slaves of sin.   (Romans 6:6)

The sin nature is gone.

So many of us have tried to get rid of this old nature.

We did not know that it was put away.

The thing called the Adamic nature is spiritual death, which had possession of our spirits.

When we are made alive, made new creations, that nature is done away.

We are tempted, and in our babyhood state, we do foolish things. That is because our bodies have never been brought into subject to our spirits.

Sin may dwell in your physical body, but it is not sin until you have consented to an act.

There is nothing wrong in your body.

Sin may lurk in your body like a demon. If there is a demon in your flesh that means your body is filled with pain and inflammation.

When that demon is cast out, your body becomes clean and healed. Sin abides in your spirit and in your mind. It does not abide in your body.

When we refer to "sin in the flesh," this means sin in the senses. It is when your senses have gained the dominion over your body.

God desires *"that you present your bodies a living sacrifice, holy, acceptable to God"* (Romans 12:1). He desires that these bodies shall be dedicated to Him after we are born again.

It is an unseemly thing for your body to rule your mind and your spirit.

You know that if you have a sore foot, that foot rules all the rest of the body.

That disease has gained the mastery so that your spirit and your mind become absolute slaves to the pain in that foot.

The same thing is true if you have an unclean appetite, a habit. That habit gains the mastery over your whole body, if you do not hold it in subjection.

The thing you say to that foot is this: "By His stripes, you are healed. In the name of Jesus, become well." (See Isaiah 53:5.)

You say to the habit that has gained the mastery over your body and mind, "You have no right to hold dominion over me any longer. In the name of Jesus Christ, depart."

You will be free.

There is only one place for sin to actually reside and that is in our spirits.

Our spirits have been recreated. The sin nature has been taken out.

We know that we have passed from death to life, because we love the brethren.   (1 John 3:14)

Satan's nature is gone. God's nature is in us. This new creation is of God. We know that we are His own.

Nothing will cripple one so quickly as to deny this truth. Nothing will establish you and build your faith as quickly as to confess it.

Confess it in your heart first.

Confess it out loud in your room. Say it over and over again: "I am a child of God. I have God's nature. I am the righteousness of God in Christ."

Say it until the words become familiar with your spirit.

Say it until your spirit and your words agree, until your whole being swings into harmony and into line with the Word of God.

That miraculous passage in Hebrews 5:13 says, *"For everyone who partakes only of milk is unskilled in the word of righteousness, for he is a babe."*

They have never sounded the depths of righteousness.

They do not know what it means to be the righteousness of God in Christ.

They do not know what it means to have God justify them and to have a standing with the Father just like Jesus's standing.

They do not seem to grasp the significance of the reality of the new creation.

That new creation is a part of God. It has partaken of God's nature. It has been made out of righteousness and holiness of truth. The new creation is not a man-made thing.

It is not a mental thing. It is a thing of God.

Just as the angel said, *"That Holy One who is to be born will be called the Son of God"* (Luke 1:35), the Holy Spirit has given birth to you and you are the holy ones of God.

You are that separated thing that belongs absolutely to the Father.

You are now His very child.

You can say, "My Father." He whispers, "My child."

For you did not receive the spirit of bondage again to fear, but you received the Spirit of adoption by whom we cry out, "Abba, Father."　　　　　　　　(Romans 8:15)

It is your continual confession of your relationship to Him and His to you that will build faith into you.

There is therefore now no condemnation to those who are in Christ Jesus.　　　　　　　　(Romans 8:1)

God is your Father, your protector, your caretaker, and your Lord.

You are in His family. Take your place. Play the part of a son.

21

FAITH AND REASON

Few of us realize that there are two kinds of knowledge in the world.

They have always been hostile to each other.

There is the knowledge that comes from our five senses: seeing, tasting, hearing, smelling, and feeling.

This is the source of all knowledge that comes to natural man.

The other kind of knowledge is a revelation knowledge. It comes from the Word.

Since educators have thrown the Word of God out of our schools, colleges, and universities, there is but one kind of knowledge taught in these institutions. That is the knowledge from the five senses.

This is suggestive, almost startling, when one thinks of it.

The mind of natural man has no way of knowing except through these avenues.

It is what we have heard, what we have tasted, what we have seen, or what we have smelled.

Astronomy comes through the eye. Down through the whole list of scientific knowledge, the same holds true. The man who only accepts sense knowledge will never know God, never understand anything connected with real Christianity because it belongs to a realm above his natural reason.

Christianity is a revelation and a miracle. The Bible is a miracle book.

The first chapter of Genesis gives us the miracle of creation.

My friend in the sense realm repudiates it and says, "It is not reasonable."

I admit he is right. It is not reasonable. It is above reason.

One of the most unhappy things that theologians have ever attempted is to square the Bible with the so-called science or reasoning from the senses.

It would have been better for them if they had tried to make science harmonize with revelation.

The understanding of revelation is purely by faith.

By faith we understand that the worlds were framed by the word of God.   (Hebrews 11:3)

You see, "*we understand*" by faith.

By faith, God said, *"Let there be"* (Genesis 1) and creation came into being. Jesus was a representative of the unseen faith of God. He walked by faith. The mighty miracles performed by Jesus were all faith miracles. The book of Acts as well as the four Gospels is a record of miracles.

The man who reads the New Testament carefully will discover that there is no place in it for human reason.

It is a miracle book.

22

FELLOWSHIP AND FAITH

Redemption had one objective: to restore man to unlimited fellowship with the Father.

You know, in human relationships, the moment that our fellowship is broken with a loved one, we lose our liberty and freedom with them.

There comes a sense of constraint.

The moment that fellowship is broken with the Father, there is a sense of constraint.

We cannot pray as we ought.

Faith is measured by our fellowship.

If we have a low type of fellowship that you will find in many homes, faith will be of a low type.

If your fellowship in the home is of a high order, your faith will be at flood tide.

The same thing is true of your heavenly Father.

If you are in perfect fellowship, loving Him, rejoicing in Him, then faith will move mountains.

But if you are under condemnation, if the sense of guilt or sin dominates your life, then your faith goes down to zero. The sense of unworthiness comes from poor fellowship.

If your prayer life sags and you have no joy in it, it is because your fellowship is broken.

Then go to Him and ask Him what the trouble is. This will usually clear up the matter.

If we confess our sins, He is faithful and just to forgive us our sins and to cleanse us from all unrighteousness.

(1 John 1:9)

When you have confessed your sins, remember they are forgiven, and when the Father forgives, He forgets.

There is no memory of it.

You dishonor Him when you remember them after they are once forgiven.

You cannot ask His forgiveness without getting it. You should then go on and live as though you have never sinned.

That is the only way you honor the blood that cleanses and the Word that gives you faith.

Rich fellowship is rich faith.

Above every other thing that you do, keep your fellowship rich and sweet.

23

FAITH'S DOMINION

Faith is dominant. Faith must rule. Reason must take its place as a helper.

The moment that reason thinks that it can assume leadership, the spiritual life of the believer begins to weaken.

Feelings must be conquered.

As long as feelings have any place in the council, faith is weakened.

Feelings must be utterly absolutely subdued, ignored. Fear must be eliminated. Faith and fear cannot associate together.

Either fear or faith rules.

Faith and fear have never been companions.

Faith and fear have never been linked up. Faith is dominant; faith is victorious; faith rules.

Fear and failure are ever linked together. Reason always wants to see, to understand.

Faith has eyes and it sees the thing done before it is begun.

It sees the dam built before a bucket of cement has been put in. It sees the desert irrigated and blooming as a rose before the blueprints are even drawn.

Faith sees with eyes that are accustomed to view the finished product, while reason's eyes see obstruction, difficulties, handicaps, human weakness, and human failings, and stands powerless in the presence of human impotence.

Faith brushes them aside, stands full-orbed, and sees them finished and completed.

Faith's highest joy is realizing a thing before it is built, entering the house and lying down on the couches of comfort before the house is even placed upon the parchment.

Faith must rule.

HOW FAITH TALKS

Faith talks in the language of God. Doubt talks in the language of man.

When I dare to say that I am what He says I am, then I am what He says I am.

What the Word says I am, I am, because He knows what He did in Christ to make me what He says I am.

The Word says that I am complete in Him. Well, God is the author of the Word. He is the author of my redemption, so if He says I am complete in Him, then I must be complete in Him.

It is barely possible that I do not understand His method of measurement.

It is barely possible that I do not understand His standards of perfection.

But I rest in what He says and I am satisfied with what He says.

What He says is what He sees in us by grace. And what He sees is what we really are.

It is not what we believe or what the church has taught us, but when He says, "We are the fullness of Him that fills all things," we are. (See Ephesians 1:23.)

When He says that He *"has blessed us with every spiritual blessing in the heavenly places in Christ"* (Ephesians 1:3), then we are blessed.

Whether we have enjoyed it or not, that is not the issue. He has blessed us.

When He declares that we are seated together with Him in the heavenlies, we are. (See Ephesians 2:6.)

Now you go about your work today, and every idle moment that you have, repeat some of these great facts over and over again.

After a while, they will become a part of you, just as the multiplication table is a part of you. Just so will this divine consciousness or Jesus consciousness become a part of you.

You cannot think God's thoughts after Him without God following His thoughts into your life and changing your thoughts into reality.

You think weakness and you are weak. You think strength and you are strong.

You think about God indwelling you and God will rise up and fill your body, His temple, with His glory.

Just as He overshadowed Solomon's temple with the cloud of His glory, so will He overshadow you.

Just as He filled that temple with His glory so that the priests could not stand to minister because of the wonder of His presence, so He will fill you today. The world's thoughts will be unable to minister in you because of the ineffable glory of His presence. Let faith speak through your lips today.

Don't talk doubts anymore. Just talk faith.

LAST WORDS

Let the world hear your confession. Every time you confess your sonship rights and your sonship place, you defeat the adversary.

Sickness has no dominion over you. Disease has no dominion over you.

Want, hunger, and need have no dominion over you. You are now in the family of plenty.

You are in the family where you lie down in green pastures and you are led by streams of sweet water.

Your soul is restored from calamity, fear, and doubt. You fellowship and commune with Him in quietness.

You are walking now in the paths of righteousness, taking advantage of your righteousness.

You are doing the works of a righteous man.

You are praying the prayers of a righteous man.

The effective, fervent prayer of a righteous man avails much.   (James 5:16)

You are praying for the sick.

You are casting out demons.

You are living a life of victory because you are the righteousness of God in Christ.

This is what we are in Christ.

ABOUT THE AUTHOR

Dr. E. W. Kenyon (1867–1948) was born in Saratoga County, New York. At age nineteen, he preached his first sermon. He pastored several churches in New England and founded the Bethel Bible Institute in Spencer, Massachusetts. This school later became the Providence Bible Institute when it was relocated to Providence, Rhode Island.

Kenyon served as an evangelist for over twenty years. In 1931, he became a pioneer in Christian radio on the Pacific Coast with his show *Kenyon's Church of the Air*, for which he earned the moniker "The Faith Builder." He also began the New Covenant Baptist Church in Seattle.

In addition to his pastoral and radio ministries, Kenyon wrote extensively. Among his books are the Bible courses *The Bible in the Light of Our Redemption: From Genesis Through Revelation* and *Studies in the Deeper Life: A Scriptural Study of Great Christian Truths,* and more than twenty other works, including *Two Kinds of Faith, In His Presence: The Secret of Prayer, The Blood Covenant, The Hidden Man, Jesus the Healer, New Creation Realities,* and *Two Kinds of Righteousness.*

All printed books by E. W. Kenyon as well as audio CDs are available from Whitaker House Publishers at www.shoptheword.com.

For more information on Kenyon's Gospel Publishing Society, as well as eBooks and MP3 audio books, please visit www.kenyons.org.

Welcome to Our House!

We Have a Special Gift for You ...

It is our privilege and pleasure to share in your love of Christian classics by publishing books that enrich your life and encourage your faith.

To show our appreciation, we invite you to sign up to receive a specially selected **Reader Appreciation Gift**, with our compliments. Just go to the Web address at the bottom of this page.

God bless you as you seek a deeper walk with Him!

WE HAVE A GIFT FOR YOU

whpub.me/classicthx

WHITAKER
HOUSE